Walking to Sleep

Books by Richard Wilbur

The Beautiful Changes and other poems

Ceremony and other poems

A Bestiary
  (editor)

Molière's The Misanthrope
  (translator)

Things of This World
  (poems)

Poems 1943–1956

Poe: Complete Poems
  (editor)

Advice to a Prophet and other poems

Molière's Tartuffe
  (translator)

The Poems of Richard Wilbur

Loudmouse
  (for children)

Shakespeare: Poems
  (editor)

Walking to Sleep
  (poems)

Richard Wilbur

WALKING TO SLEEP

New Poems and Translations

A Harvest Book

Harcourt Brace Jovanovich, Inc.

New York

"On the Marginal Way," "Complaint," "Seed Leaves," "A Wood," "Running," "Walking to Sleep," "In a Churchyard," "In the Field," "Thyme Flowering among Rocks," and "A Late Aubade" appeared originally in *The New Yorker;* "François Villon: Ballade of the Ladies of Time Past" in *Poetry.* The translations from the Russian of Andrei Voznesensky are reprinted with the permission of the publishers of *Antiworlds,* edited by Patricia Blake and Max Hayward, © 1966 by Basic Books, Inc., Publishers, New York. Others appeared originally in *The Atlantic Monthly, Encounter, A Festschrift for Marianne Moore's Seventy-Seventh Birthday, Hispanic Arts, The Hudson Review, Kayak, The Nation, The New York Review of Books, The Paris Review, Penny Poems from Midwestern University, Poetry Northwest, The Quarterly Review of Literature,* and *The Tin Drum.*

For my Mother and my Father

Contents

II
Thyme

III
Walking to Sleep

IV
Translations

I
In the Field

The Lilacs

Those laden lilacs
                    at the lawn's end
Came stark, spindly,
                    and in staggered file,
Like walking wounded
                    from the dead of winter.
We watched them waken
                    in the brusque weather
To rot and rootbreak,
                    to ripped branches,
And saw them shiver
                    as the memory swept them
Of night and numbness
                    and the taste of nothing.
Out of present pain
                    and from past terror
Their bullet-shaped buds
                    came quick and bursting,
As if they aimed
                    to be open with us!

But the sun suddenly
                    settled about them,
And green and grateful
                    the lilacs grew,

Healed in that hush,
                    that hospital quiet.
These lacquered leaves
                    where the light paddles
And the big blooms
                    buzzing among them
Have kept their counsel,
                    conveying nothing
Of their mortal message,
                    unless one should measure
The depth and dumbness
                    of death's kingdom
By the pure power
                    of this perfume.

On the Marginal Way
for J. C. P.

Another cove of shale,
But the beach here is rubbled with strange rock
   That is sleek, fluent, and taffy-pale.
I stare, reminded with a little shock
How, by a shore in Spain, George Borrow saw
A hundred women basking in the raw.

They must have looked like this,
That catch of bodies on the sand, that strew
   Of rondure, crease, and orifice,
Lap, flank, and knee—a too abundant view
Which, though he'd had the lenses of a fly,
Could not have waked desire in Borrow's eye.

Has the light altered now?
The rocks flush rose and have the melting shape
   Of bodies fallen anyhow.
It is a Géricault of blood and rape,
Some desert town despoiled, some caravan
Pillaged, its people murdered to a man,

And those who murdered them
Galloping off, a rumpling line of dust
   Like the wave's white, withdrawing hem.
But now the vision of a colder lust

Clears, as the wind goes chill and all is greyed
By a swift cloud that drags a carrion shade.

    If these are bodies still,
Theirs is a death too dead to look asleep,
    Like that of Auschwitz' final kill,
Poor slaty flesh abandoned in a heap
And then, like sea-rocks buried by a wave,
Bulldozed at last into a common grave.

    It is not tricks of sense
But the time's fright within me which distracts
    Least fancies into violence
And makes my thought take cover in the facts,
As now it does, remembering how the bed
Of layered rock two miles above my head

    Hove ages up and broke
Soundless asunder, when the shrinking skin
    Of Earth, blacked out by steam and smoke,
Gave passage to the muddled fire within,
Its crannies flooding with a sweat of quartz,
And lathered magmas out of deep retorts

Welled up, as here, to fill
With tumbled rockmeal, stone-fume, lithic spray,
   The dike's brief chasm and the sill.
Weathered until the sixth and human day
By sanding winds and water, scuffed and brayed
By the slow glacier's heel, these forms were made

   That now recline and burn
Comely as Eve and Adam, near a sea
   Transfigured by the sun's return.
And now three girls lie golden in the lee
Of a great arm or thigh, and are as young
As the bright boulders that they lie among.

   Though, high above the shore
On someone's porch, spread wings of newsprint flap
   The tidings of some dirty war,
It is a perfect day: the waters clap
Their hands and kindle, and the gull in flight
Loses himself at moments, white in white,

   And like a breaking thought
Joy for a moment floods into the mind,

Blurting that all things shall be brought
To the full state and stature of their kind,
By what has found the manhood of this stone.
May that vast motive wash and wash our own.

Complaint

*In reality, each love is that of the divine image,
and each is pure.*   FICINO

Why is it that whenever I talk with the duchess
My belly growls and my nose waters? Why must it
Be my hand that tumbles her wine-glass over
Into the Cellini salt-dish?

Stiff as a gaffer, fidgety as a child,
After twenty years of struggling to be a courtier
I remain incapable of the least politeness,
Wit, song, or learning,

And I wonder sometimes, what is it in me that hates me?
Is it that rolling captain who should burst
Like surf into her presence, dumping down
His pillage of the seas,

And in a wink dissolve her castled pride?
She scorns no common magic, and could be pleased
To be manhandled like a kitchen-girl,
So it were sweet and reckless.

Or is it that idolatrous fool that's in me,
Who, lest she alter, should enchant the hour
With gentled sparrows and an aimless lute,
Enthralling her with tales

Of a king's daughter bound in mountain sleep,
Whose prince and wakener, detained by trials
In deserts, deeps, and grottoes of the world,
Approaches her forever?

Or am I spited by the priest I might be
There in the stone grove of her oratory?
No ship sails out so free as she at prayer,
With head bowed and shrouded.

Confessing her, and my delight in her,
To the great ways and haven of her beauty,
Would I not serve her better? Would not my hand
Be steady with the wine?

Jackass, again you turn and turn this prism,
Whose every light is of the purest water.
How should I fathom her whose white hands fold
The rainbow like a fan?

O maiden, muse, and maiden, O my love
Whose every moment is the quick of time,
I am your bumbling servant now and ever,
In this and the other kingdom.

Fern-Beds in Hampshire County

Although from them
Steep stands of beech and sugar-maple stem,
Varied with birch, or ash, or basswood trees
Which spring will throng with bees,
While intervening thickets grow complex
With flower, seed, and variance of sex,
And the whole wood conspires, by change of kind,
To break the purchase of the gathering mind,
The ferns are as they were.
Let but a trifling stir
Of air traverse their pools or touchy beds
And some will dip their heads,
Some switch a moment like a scribbling quill
And then be still,
Sporadic as in guarded bays
The rockweed slaps a bit, or sways.
Then let the wind grow bluff, and though
The sea lies far to eastward, far below,
These fluent spines, with whipped pale underside,
Will climb through timber as a smoking tide
Through pier-stakes, beat their sprays about the base
Of every boulder, scale its creviced face
And, wave on wave, like some green infantry,
Storm all the slope as high as eye can see.
Whatever at the heart

Of creatures makes them branch and burst apart,
Or at the core of star or tree may burn
At last to turn
And make an end of time,
These airy plants, tenacious of their prime,
Dwell in the swept recurrence of
An ancient conquest, shaken by first love
As when they answered to the boomed command
That the sea's green rise up and take the land.

In a Churchyard

That flower unseen, that gem of purest ray,
Bright thoughts uncut by men:
Strange that you need but speak them, Thomas Gray,
And the mind skips and dives beyond its ken,

Finding at once the wild supposèd bloom,
Or in the imagined cave
Some pulse of crystal staving off the gloom
As covertly as phosphorus in a grave.

Void notions proper to a buried head!
Beneath these tombstones here
Unseenness fills the sockets of the dead,
Whatever to their souls may now appear;

And who but those unfathomably deaf
Who quiet all this ground
Could catch, within the ear's diminished clef,
A music innocent of time and sound?

What do the living hear, then, when the bell
Hangs plumb within the tower
Of the still church, and still their thoughts compel
Pure tollings that intend no mortal hour?

As when a ferry for the shore of death
Glides looming toward the dock,
Her engines cut, her spirits bating breath
As the ranked pilings narrow toward the shock,

So memory and expectation set
Some pulseless clangor free
Of circumstance, and charm us to forget
This twilight crumbling in the churchyard tree,

Those swifts or swallows which do not pertain,
Scuffed voices in the drive,
That light flicked on behind the vestry pane,
Till, unperplexed from all that is alive,

It shadows all our thought, balked imminence
Of uncommitted sound,
And still would tower at the sill of sense
Were not, as now, its honed abeyance crowned

With a mauled boom of summons far more strange
Than any stroke unheard,
Which breaks again with unimagined range
Through all reverberations of the word,

Pooling the mystery of things that are,
The buzz of prayer said,
The scent of grass, the earliest-blooming star,
These unseen gravestones, and the darker dead.

Seed Leaves

Homage to R. F.

Here something stubborn comes,
Dislodging the earth crumbs
And making crusty rubble.
It comes up bending double,
And looks like a green staple.
It could be seedling maple,
Or artichoke, or bean.
That remains to be seen.

Forced to make choice of ends,
The stalk in time unbends,
Shakes off the seed-case, heaves
Aloft, and spreads two leaves
Which still display no sure
And special signature.
Toothless and fat, they keep
The oval form of sleep.

This plant would like to grow
And yet be embryo;
Increase, and yet escape
The doom of taking shape;
Be vaguely vast, and climb
To the tip end of time
With all of space to fill,

Like boundless Igdrasil
That has the stars for fruit.

But something at the root
More urgent than that urge
Bids two true leaves emerge,
And now the plant, resigned
To being self-defined
Before it can commerce
With the great universe,
Takes aim at all the sky
And starts to ramify.

In the Field

This field-grass brushed our legs
Last night, when out we stumbled looking up,
   Wading as through the cloudy dregs
     Of a wide, sparkling cup,

   Our thrown-back heads aswim
In the grand, kept appointments of the air,
   Save where a pine at the sky's rim
     Took something from the Bear.

   Black in her glinting chains,
Andromeda feared nothing from the seas,
   Preserved as by no hero's pains,
     Or hushed Euripides',

   And there the dolphin glowed,
Still flailing through a diamond froth of stars,
   Flawless as when Arion rode
     One of its avatars.

   But none of that was true.
What shapes that Greece or Babylon discerned
   Had time not slowly drawn askew
     Or like cat's cradles turned?

And did we not recall
That Egypt's north was in the Dragon's tail?
  As if a form of type should fall
    And dash itself like hail,

  The heavens jumped away,
Bursting the cincture of the zodiac,
  Shot flares with nothing left to say
    To us, not coming back

  Unless they should at last,
Like hard-flung dice that ramble out the throw,
  Be gathered for another cast.
    Whether that might be so

  We could not say, but trued
Our talk awhile to words of the real sky,
  Chatting of class or magnitude,
    Star-clusters, nebulae,

  And how Antares, huge
As Mars' big roundhouse swing, and more, was fled
  As in some rimless centrifuge
    Into a blink of red.

It was the nip of fear
That told us when imagination caught
   The feel of what we said, came near
      The schoolbook thoughts we thought,

      And faked a scan of space
Blown black and hollow by our spent grenade,
   All worlds dashed out without a trace,
      The very light unmade.

      Then, in the late-night chill,
We turned and picked our way through outcrop stone
   By the faint starlight, up the hill
      To where our bed-lamp shone.

      Today, in the same field,
The sun takes all, and what could lie beyond?
   Those holes in heaven have been sealed
      Like rain-drills in a pond,

      And we, beheld in gold,
See nothing starry but these galaxies
   Of flowers, dense and manifold,
      Which lift about our knees—

White daisy-drifts where you
Sink down to pick an armload as we pass,
    Sighting the heal-all's minor blue
        In chasms of the grass,

And strews of hawkweed where,
Amongst the reds or yellows as they burn,
    A few dead polls commit to air
        The seeds of their return.

We could no doubt mistake
These flowers for some answer to that fright
    We felt for all creation's sake
        In our dark talk last night,

Taking to heart what came
Of the heart's wish for life, which, staking here
    In the least field an endless claim,
        Beats on from sphere to sphere

And pounds beyond the sun,
Where nothing less peremptory can go,
    And is ourselves, and is the one
        Unbounded thing we know.

A Wood

Some would distinguish nothing here but oaks,
Proud heads conversant with the power and glory
Of heaven's rays or heaven's thunderstrokes,
And adumbrators to the understory,
Where, in their shade, small trees of modest leanings
Contend for light and are content with gleanings.

And yet here's dogwood: overshadowed, small,
But not inclined to droop and count its losses,
It cranes its way to sunlight after all,
And signs the air of May with Maltese crosses.
And here's witch hazel, that from underneath
Great vacant boughs will bloom in winter's teeth.

Given a source of light so far away
That nothing, short or tall, comes very near it,
Would it not take a proper fool to say
That any tree has not the proper spirit?
Air, water, earth and fire are to be blended,
But no one style, I think, is recommended.

For Dudley

Even when death has taken
An exceptional man,
It is common things which touch us, gathered
In the house that proved a hostel.

Though on his desk there lie
The half of a sentence
Not to be finished by us, who lack
His gaiety, his Greek,

It is the straight back
Of a good woman
Which now we notice. For her guests' hunger
She sets the polished table.

And now the quick sun,
Rounding the gable,
Picks out a chair, a vase of flowers,
Which had stood till then in shadow.

It is the light of which
Achilles spoke,
Himself a shadow then, recalling
The splendor of mere being.

As if we were perceived
From a black ship—
A small knot of island folk,
The Light-Dwellers, pouring

A life to the dark sea—
All that we do
Is touched with ocean, yet we remain
On the shore of what we know.

We say that we are behaving
As he would have us—
He who was brave and loved this world,
Who did not hold with weeping,

Yet in the mind as in
The shut closet
Where his coats hang in black procession,
There is a covert muster.

One is moved to turn to him,
The exceptional man,
Telling him all these things, and waiting
For the deft, lucid answer.

At the sound of that voice's deep
Specific silence,
The sun winks and fails in the window.
Light perpetual keep him.

Running

I. 1933

(North Caldwell, New Jersey)

What were we playing? Was it prisoner's base?
I ran with whacking keds
Down the cart-road past Rickard's place,
And where it dropped beside the tractor-sheds

Leapt out into the air above a blurred
Terrain, through jolted light,
Took two hard lopes, and at the third
Spanked off a hummock-side exactly right,

And made the turn, and with delighted strain
Sprinted across the flat
By the bull-pen, and up the lane.
Thinking of happiness, I think of that.

II. PATRIOTS' DAY

(Wellesley, Massachusetts)

Restless that noble day, appeased by soft
Drinks and tobacco, littering the grass
While the flag snapped and brightened far aloft,
We waited for the marathon to pass,

We fathers and our little sons, let out
Of school and office to be put to shame.
Now from the street-side someone raised a shout,
And into view the first small runners came.

Dark in the glare, they seemed to thresh in place
Like preening flies upon a window-sill,
Yet gained and grew, and at a cruel pace
Swept by us on their way to Heartbreak Hill—

Legs driving, fists at port, clenched faces, men,
And in amongst them, stamping on the sun,
Our champion Kelley, who would win again,
Rocked in his will, at rest within his run.

III. DODWELLS ROAD
(*Cummington, Massachusetts*)

I jog up out of the woods
To the crown of the road, and slow to a swagger there,
The wind harsh and cool to my throat,
A good ache in my rib-cage.

Loud burden of streams at run-off,
And the sun's rocket frazzled in blown tree-heads:
Still I am part of that great going,
Though I stroll now, and am watchful.

Where the road turns and debouches,
The land sinks westward into exhausted pasture.
From fields which yield to aspen now
And pine at last will shadow,

Boy-shouts reach me, and barking.
What is the thing which men will not surrender?
It is what they have never had, I think,
Or missed in its true season,

So that their thoughts turn in
At the same roadhouse nightly, the same cloister,
The wild mouth of the same brave river
Never now to be charted.

You, whoever you are,
If you want to walk with me you must step lively.
I run, too, when the mood offers,
Though the god of that has left me.

But why in the hell spoil it?
I make a clean gift of my young running
To the two boys who break into view,
Hurdling the rocks and racing,

Their dog dodging before them
This way and that, his yaps flushing a pheasant
Who lifts now from the blustery grass
Flying full tilt already.

Under Cygnus

Who says I shall not straighten till I bend,
And must be broken if I hope to mend?
Did Samson gain by being chained and blind?
Dark heaven hints at something of the kind,
Seeing that as we beat toward Hercules
Our flank is compassed by the galaxy's,
And we drawn off from our intended course
By a grand reel of stars whose banded force,
Catching us up, makes light of all our loss,
And dances us into the Northern Cross.

Well, if I must surrender and be gay
In the wrong pasture of the Milky Way,
If in the Cross I must resign my Sword,
To hang among the trophies of the Lord,
Let my distinction not consist alone
In having let myself be overthrown.
It was my loves and labors, carried high,
Which drove the flight that heaven turns awry,
My dreams which told the stars what they should tell.
Let the Swan, dying, sing of that as well.

II
Thyme

Thyme Flowering among Rocks

This, if Japanese,
Would represent grey boulders
Walloped by rough seas

So that, here or there,
The balked water tossed its froth
Straight into the air.

Here, where things are what
They are, it is thyme blooming,
Rocks, and nothing but—

Having, nonetheless,
Many small leaves implicit,
A green countlessness.

Crouching down, peering
Into perplexed recesses,
You find a clearing

Occupied by sun
Where, along prone, rachitic
Branches, one by one,

Pale stems arise, squared
In the manner of *Mentha,*
The oblong leaves paired.

One branch, in ending,
Lifts a little and begets
A straight-ascending

Spike, whorled with fine blue
Or purple trumpets, banked in
The leaf-axils. You

Are lost now in dense
Fact, fact which one might have thought
Hidden from the sense,

Blinking at detail
Peppery as this fragrance,
Lost to proper scale

As, in the motion
Of striped fins, a bathysphere
Forgets the ocean.

It makes the craned head
Spin. Unfathomed thyme! The world's
A dream, Basho said,

Not because that dream's
A falsehood, but because it's
Truer than it seems.

A Miltonic Sonnet for Mr. Johnson
on His Refusal of Peter Hurd's Official Portrait

Heir to the office of a man not dead
Who drew our Declaration up, who planned
Range and Rotunda with his drawing-hand
And harbored Palestrina in his head,
Who would have wept to see small nations dread
The imposition of our cattle-brand,
With public truth at home mistold or banned,
And in whose term no army's blood was shed,

Rightly you say the picture is too large
Which Peter Hurd by your appointment drew,
And justly call that Capitol too bright
Which signifies our people in your charge;
Wait, Sir, and see how time will render you,
Who talk of vision but are weak of sight.

6 January 1967

A Riddle

For M. M.

Where far in forest I am laid,
In a place ringed around by stones,
Look for no melancholy shade,
And have no thoughts of buried bones;
For I am bodiless and bright,
And fill this glade with sudden glow;
The leaves are washed in under-light;
Shade lies upon the boughs like snow.

Playboy

High on his stockroom ladder like a dunce
The stock-boy sits, and studies like a sage
The subject matter of one glossy page,
As lost in curves as Archimedes once.

Sometimes, without a glance, he feeds himself.
The left hand, like a mother-bird in flight,
Brings him a sandwich for a sidelong bite,
And then returns it to a dusty shelf.

What so engrosses him? The wild décor
Of this pink-papered alcove into which
A naked girl has stumbled, with its rich
Welter of pelts and pillows on the floor,

Amidst which, kneeling in a supple pose,
She lifts a goblet in her farther hand,
As if about to toast a flower-stand
Above which hovers an exploding rose

Fired from a long-necked crystal vase that rests
Upon a tasseled and vermilion cloth
One taste of which would shrivel up a moth?
Or is he pondering her perfect breasts?

Nothing escapes him of her body's grace
Or of her floodlit skin, so sleek and warm
And yet so strangely like a uniform,
But what now grips his fancy is her face,

And how the cunning picture holds her still
At just that smiling instant when her soul,
Grown sweetly faint, and swept beyond control,
Consents to his inexorable will.

The Mechanist

Advancing with a self-denying gaze, he
Looks closely at the love-divining daisy.

Since none but persons may of persons learn,
The frightened plant denies herself in turn,

And sways away as if to flee her fears,
Clashing her flower heads like clumsy gears.

The Agent

Behind his back, the first wave passes over
The city which at dawn he left for good,
His staff-car musing through the streets, its tires
Kissing the rainy cheeks of cobblestones,
Till at St. Basil's gate the tower clock
Roused with a groan, flung down the hour, and shook
The tears into his eyes. In those lapped roars
And souring resonance he heard as well
Hoarse trains that highball down the world's ravines,
Some boat-horn's whoop and shudder, all sick thrills
Of transit and forsaking. Now he is calm,
Here in this locust-copse, his rendezvous,
Laying his uniform away in leaves
For good, and lacing up a peasant jerkin.
The sky fills with a suave bombination
Of yet more planes in level swarm; the city
Rocks now with flash and thud; the guildhall windows
Blink him a leaden message, that the small
Park, with its fountains, where his custom was
To sip a *fine* and watch the *passeggiata,*
Is deep in rubble and its trees afire.
But still he looks away, less now from grief
Than from a fuddled lostness how unlike
The buoyant spirits of his coming, when,
Light as a milkweed-puff, his parachute

Fell swaying toward a flashlight in a field
Of moonlit grain, which softly hove to meet him.
Bedded that night amongst the bins and kegs
Of a damp cellar, he did not rehearse
His orders, or the fear that some small flaw
In his forged self or papers might betray him,
But lay rejoicing in the smell of roots
And age, as in a painted cart next morning,
Hid under hay, he listened to the ching
Of harness and the sound of rim-struck stones.
And then that train-ride!—all compartments filled
With folk returning from the holiday,
From bonfire-jumping, dancing in a round,
And tying amulets of mistletoe.
Like some collector steeped in catalogues
Who finds at last in some dim shop or attic
A Martinique *tête-bêche* imperforate
Or still unbroken egg by Fabergé,
He took possession, prizing the foreknown
Half-Tartar eyes, the slurring of the schwa,
The braids and lederhosen, and the near-
Telepathy of shrugs and eyebrow-cockings
In which the nuance of their speeches lay.
Rocked by the train, with festal smiles about him,
His belly warmed by proffered *akvavit*,

He felt his hands fill with authentic gestures:
He would not shift his fork from left to right,
Nor bless himself right-shoulder-foremost. Born
Not of a culture but a drafty state,
And having, therefore, little to unlearn,
He would put on with ease the tribal ways
And ritual demeanors of this land
Toward whose chief city he was chugging now
To savor and betray.

             But now a torn
Blare, like the clearing of a monstrous throat,
Rolls from those fields which vanish toward the border;
Dark tanks and half-tracks come, breasting the wheat,
And after them, in combat scatterment,
Dark infantry. He can already spy
Their cold familiar eyes, their bodies heavy
With the bulk foods of home, and so remembers
A gravel playground full of lonely wind,
The warmth of a wet bed. How hard it is,
He thinks, to be cheated of a fated life
In a deep *patria,* and so to be
A foundling never lost, a pure impostor
Faithless to everything. An ill thought strikes him:
What if these soldiers, through some chance or blunder,

Have not been briefed about him and his mission?
What will they make of him—a nervous man
In farmer's costume, speaking a precious accent,
Who cannot name the streets of his own town?
Would they not, after all, be right to shoot him?
He shrinks against a trunk and waits to see.

The Proof

Shall I love God for causing me to be?
I was mere utterance; shall these words love me?

Yet when I caused his work to jar and stammer,
And one free subject loosened all his grammar,

I love him that he did not in a rage
Once and forever rule me off the page,

But, thinking I might come to please him yet,
Crossed out *delete* and wrote his patient *stet*.

A Late Aubade

You could be sitting now in a carrel
Turning some liver-spotted page,
Or rising in an elevator-cage
Toward Ladies' Apparel.

You could be planting a raucous bed
Of salvia, in rubber gloves,
Or lunching through a screed of someone's loves
With pitying head,

Or making some unhappy setter
Heel, or listening to a bleak
Lecture on Schoenberg's serial technique.
Isn't this better?

Think of all the time you are not
Wasting, and would not care to waste,
Such things, thank God, not being to your taste.
Think what a lot

Of time, by woman's reckoning,
You've saved, and so may spend on this,
You who had rather lie in bed and kiss
Than anything.

It's almost noon, you say? If so,
Time flies, and I need not rehearse
The rosebuds-theme of centuries of verse.
If you *must* go,

Wait for a while, then slip downstairs
And bring us up some chilled white wine,
And some blue cheese, and crackers, and some fine
Ruddy-skinned pears.

Matthew VIII, 28 ff.

Rabbi, we Gadarenes
Are not ascetics; we are fond of wealth and possessions.
Love, as you call it, we obviate by means
Of the planned release of aggressions.

We have deep faith in prosperity.
Soon, it is hoped, we will reach our full potential.
In the light of our gross product, the practice of charity
Is palpably inessential.

It is true that we go insane;
That for no good reason we are possessed by devils;
That we suffer, despite the amenities which obtain
At all but the lowest levels.

We shall not, however, resign
Our trust in the high-heaped table and the full trough.
If you cannot cure us without destroying our swine,
We had rather you shoved off.

For K. R. on Her Sixtieth Birthday

Blow out the candles of your cake.
They will not leave you in the dark,
Who round with grace this dusky arc
Of the grand tour which souls must take.

You who have sounded William Blake,
And the still pool, to Plato's mark,
Blow out the candles of your cake.
They will not leave you in the dark.

Yet, for your friends' benighted sake,
Detain your upward-flying spark;
Get us that wish, though like the lark
You whet your wings till dawn shall break:
Blow out the candles of your cake.

III
Walking to Sleep

Walking to Sleep

As a queen sits down, knowing that a chair will be there,
Or a general raises his hand and is given the field-glasses,
Step off assuredly into the blank of your mind.
Something will come to you. Although at first
You nod through nothing like a fogbound prow,
Gravel will breed in the margins of your gaze,
Perhaps with tussocks or a dusty flower,
And, humped like dolphins playing in the bow-wave,
Hills will suggest themselves. All such suggestions
Are yours to take or leave, but hear this warning:
Let them not be too velvet green, the fields
Which the deft needle of your eye appoints,
Nor the old farm past which you make your way
Too shady-linteled, too instinct with home.
It is precisely from Potemkin barns
With their fresh-painted hex signs on the gables,
Their sparkling gloom within, their stanchion-rattle
And sweet breath of silage, that there comes
The trotting cat whose head is but a skull.
Try to remember this: what you project
Is what you will perceive; what you perceive
With any passion, be it love or terror,
May take on whims and powers of its own.
Therefore a numb and grudging circumspection
Will serve you best, unless you overdo it,

Watching your step too narrowly, refusing
To specify a world, shrinking your purview
To a tight vision of your inching shoes—
Which may, as soon you come to think, be crossing
An unseen gorge upon a rotten trestle.
What you must manage is to bring to mind
A landscape not worth looking at, some bleak
Champaign at dead November's end, its grass
As dry as lichen, and its lichens grey,
Such glumly simple country that a glance
Of flat indifference from time to time
Will stabilize it. Lifeless thus, and leafless,
The view should set at rest all thoughts of ambush.
Nevertheless, permit no roadside thickets
Which, as you pass, might shake with worse than wind;
Revoke all trees and other cover; blast
The upstart boulder which a flicking shape
Has stepped behind; above all, put a stop
To the known stranger up ahead, whose face
Half turns to mark you with a creased expression.
Here let me interject that steady trudging
Can make you drowsy, so that without transition,
As when an old film jumps in the projector,
You will be wading a dun hallway, rounding
A newel post, and starting up the stairs.

Should that occur, adjust to circumstances
And carry on, taking these few precautions:
Detach some portion of your thought to guard
The outside of the building; as you wind
From room to room, leave nothing at your back,
But slough all memories at every threshold;
Nor must you dream of opening any door
Until you have foreseen what lies beyond it.
Regardless of its seeming size, or what
May first impress you as its style or function,
The abrupt structure which involves you now
Will improvise like vapor. Groping down
The gritty cellar steps and past the fuse-box,
Brushing through sheeted lawn-chairs, you emerge
In some cathedral's pillared crypt, and thence,
Your brow alight with carbide, pick your way
To the main shaft through drifts and rubbly tunnels.
Promptly the hoist, ascending toward the pit-head,
Rolls downward past your gaze a dinted rock-face
Peppered with hacks and drill-holes, which acquire
Insensibly the look of hieroglyphics.
Whether to surface now within the vast
Stone tent where Cheops lay secure, or take
The proffered shed of corrugated iron
Which gives at once upon a vacant barracks,

Is up to you. Need I, at this point, tell you
What to avoid? Avoid the pleasant room
Where someone, smiling to herself, has placed
A bowl of yellow freesias. Do not let
The thought of her in yellow, lithe and sleek
As lemonwood, mislead you where the curtains,
Romping like spinnakers which taste the wind,
Bellying out and lifting till the sill
Has shipped a drench of sunlight, then subsiding,
Both warm and cool the love-bed. Your concern
Is not to be detained by dread, or by
Such dear acceptances as would entail it,
But to pursue an ever-dimming course
Of pure transition, treading as in water
Past crumbling tufa, down cloacal halls
Of boarded-up hotels, through attics full
Of glassy taxidermy, moping on
Like a drugged fire-inspector. What you hope for
Is that at some point of the pointless journey,
Indoors or out, and when you least expect it,
Right in the middle of your stride, like that,
So neatly that you never feel a thing,
The kind assassin Sleep will draw a bead
And blow your brains out.

What, are you still awake?
Then you must risk another tack and footing.
Forget what I have said. Open your eyes
To the good blackness not of your room alone
But of the sky you trust is over it,
Whose stars, though foundering in the time to come,
Bequeath us constantly a jetsam beauty.
Now with your knuckles rub your eyelids, seeing
The phosphenes caper like St. Elmo's fire,
And let your head heel over on the pillow
Like a flung skiff on wild Gennesaret.
Let all things storm your thought with the moiled flocking
Of startled rookeries, or flak in air,
Or blossom-fall, and out of that come striding
In the strong dream by which you have been chosen.
Are you upon the roads again? If so,
Be led past honeyed meadows which might tempt
A wolf to graze, and groves which are not you
But answer to your suppler self, that nature
Able to bear the thrush's quirky glee
In stands of chuted light, yet praise as well,
All leaves aside, the barren bark of winter.
When, as you may, you find yourself approaching
A crossroads and its laden gallows tree,

Do not with hooded eyes allow the shadow
Of a man moored in air to bruise your forehead,
But lift your gaze and stare your brother down,
Though the swart crows have pecked his sockets hollow.
As for what turn your travels then will take,
I cannot guess. Long errantry perhaps
Will arm you to be gentle, or the claws
Of nightmare flap you pathless God knows where,
As the crow flies, to meet your dearest horror.
Still, if you are in luck, you may be granted,
As, inland, one can sometimes smell the sea,
A moment's perfect carelessness, in which
To stumble a few steps and sink to sleep
In the same clearing where, in the old story,
A holy man discovered Vishnu sleeping,
Wrapped in his maya, dreaming by a pool
On whose calm face all images whatever
Lay clear, unfathomed, taken as they came.

IV
Translations

Compass

All things are words of some strange tongue, in thrall
To Someone, Something, who both day and night
Proceeds in endless gibberish to write
The history of the world. In that dark scrawl

Rome is set down, and Carthage, I, you, all,
And this my being which escapes me quite,
My anguished life that's cryptic, recondite,
And garbled as the tongues of Babel's fall.

Beyond the name there lies what has no name;
Today I have felt its shadow stir the aim
Of this blue needle, light and keen, whose sweep

Homes to the utmost of the sea its love,
Suggestive of a watch in dreams, or of
Some bird, perhaps, who shifts a bit in sleep.

JORGE LUIS BORGES:
Everness

One thing does not exist: Oblivion.
God saves the metal and he saves the dross,
And his prophetic memory guards from loss
The moons to come, and those of evenings gone.
Everything *is:* the shadows in the glass
Which, in between the day's two twilights, you
Have scattered by the thousands, or shall strew
Henceforward in the mirrors that you pass.
And everything is part of that diverse
Crystalline memory, the universe;
Whoever through its endless mazes wanders
Hears door on door click shut behind his stride,
And only from the sunset's farther side
Shall view at last the Archetypes and the Splendors.

Ewigkeit

Turn on my tongue, O Spanish verse; confirm
Once more what Spanish verse has always said
Since Seneca's black Latin; speak your dread
Sentence that all is fodder for the worm.
Come, celebrate once more pale ash, pale dust,
The pomps of death and the triumphant crown
Of that bombastic queen who tramples down
The petty banners of our pride and lust.
Enough of that. What things have blessed my clay
Let me not cravenly deny. The one
Word of no meaning is Oblivion,
And havened in eternity, I know,
My many precious losses burn and stay:
That forge, that night, that risen moon aglow.

ANNA AKHMATOVA:
Lot's Wife

The just man followed then his angel guide
Where he strode on the black highway, hulking and bright;
But a wild grief in his wife's bosom cried,
Look back, it is not too late for a last sight

Of the red towers of your native Sodom, the square
Where once you sang, the gardens you shall mourn,
And the tall house with empty windows where
You loved your husband and your babes were born.

She turned, and looking on the bitter view
Her eyes were welded shut by mortal pain;
Into transparent salt her body grew,
And her quick feet were rooted in the plain.

Who would waste tears upon her? Is she not
The least of our losses, this unhappy wife?
Yet in my heart she will not be forgot
Who, for a single glance, gave up her life.

ANDREI VOZNESENSKY:
Foggy Street

The air is grey-white as a pigeon-feather.
      Police bob up like corks on a fishing-net.
Foggy weather.
What century is it? What era? I forget.

As in a nightmare, everything is crumbling;
      people have come unsoldered; nothing's intact.
I plod on, stumbling,
Or flounder in cotton wool, to be more exact.

Noses. Parking-lights. Badges flash and blur.
      All's vague, as at a magic-lantern show.
Your hat-check, Sir?
Mustn't walk off with the wrong head, you know.

It's as if a woman who's scarcely left your lips
      Should blur in the mind, yet trouble it with recall—
Bereft now, widowed by your love's eclipse—
Still yours, yet suddenly not yours at all . . .

Can that be Venus? No—an ice-cream vendor!
      I bump into curbstones, bump into passersby.
Are they friends, I wonder?
Home-bred Iagos, how covert you are, how sly!

Why it's you, my darling, shivering there alone!
    Your overcoat's too big for you, my dear.
But why have you grown
That moustache? Why is there frost in your hairy ear?

I trip, I stagger, I persist.
    Murk, murk . . . there's nothing visible anywhere.
Whose is the cheek you brush now in the mist?
Ahoy there!
One's voice won't carry in this heavy air.

When the fog lifts, how brilliant it is, how rare!

ANDREI VOZNESENSKY:
Antiworlds

The clerk Bukashkin is our neighbor:
His face is grey as blotting-paper.

But like balloons of blue or red,
Bright Antiworlds
      float over his head!
On them reposes, prestidigitous,
Ruling the cosmos, a demon-magician,
Anti-Bukashkin the academician,
Lapped in the arms of Lollobrigidas.

But Anti-Bukashkin's dreams are the color
Of blotting-paper, and couldn't be duller.

Long live Antiworlds! They rebut
With dreams the rat-race and the rut.
For some to be clever, some must be boring.
No deserts? No oases, then.
There are no women—
      just anti-men.
In the forests, anti-machines are roaring.
There's the dirt of the earth, as well as the salt.
If the earth broke down, the sun would halt.

Ah, my critics; how I love them.
Upon the neck of the keenest of them,
Fragrant and bald as fresh-baked bread,
There shines a perfect anti-head . . .

. . . I sleep with windows open wide;
Somewhere a falling star invites,
And skyscrapers,
                          like stalactites,
Hang from the planet's underside.
There, upside down
                          below me far,
Stuck like a fork into the earth,
Or perching like a carefree moth,
My little Antiworld,
                          there you are!

In the middle of the night, why is it
That Antiworlds are moved to visit?

Why do they sit together, gawking
At the television, and never talking?

Between them, not one word has passed.
Their first strange meeting is their last.

Neither can manage the least *bon ton*.
Oh, how they'll blush for it later on!

Their ears are burning like a pair
Of crimson butterflies, hovering there . . .

. . . A distinguished lecturer lately told me,
"Antiworlds are a total loss."

Still, my apartment-cell won't hold me;
I thrash in my sleep, I turn and toss.

And, radio-like, my cat lies curled
With his green eye tuned in to the world.

ANDREI VOZNESENSKY:
Dead Still

Now, with your palms on the blades of my shoulders,
Let us embrace:
Let there be only your lips' breath on my face,
Only, behind our backs, the plunge of rollers.

Our backs, which like two shells in moonlight shine,
Are shut behind us now;
We lie here huddled, listening brow to brow,
Like life's twin formula or double sign.

In folly's world-wide wind
Our shoulders shield from the weather
The calm we now beget together,
Like a flame held between hand and hand.

Does each cell have a soul within it?
If so, fling open all your little doors,
And all your souls shall flutter like the linnet
In the cages of my pores.

Nothing is hidden that shall not be known.
Yet by no storm of scorn shall we
Be pried from this embrace, and left alone
Like muted shells forgetful of the sea.

Meanwhile, O load of stress and bother,
Lie on the shells of our backs in a great heap!
It will but press us closer, one to the other.

We are asleep.

Rondeau

The year has cast its cloak away
That was of driving rains and snows,
And now in flowered arras goes,
And wears the clear sun's glossy ray.

No bird or beast but seems to say
In cries or chipper tremolos:
The year has cast its cloak away
That was of driving rains and snows.

Stream, brook and silver fountain play,
And each upon itself bestows
A spangled livery as it flows.
All creatures are in fresh array.
The year has cast its cloak away.

Ballade of the Ladies of Time Past

O tell me where, in lands or seas,
Flora, that Roman belle, has strayed,
Thais, or Archipiades,
Who put each other in the shade,
Or Echo who by bank and glade
Gave back the crying of the hound,
And whose sheer beauty could not fade.
But where shall last year's snow be found?

Where too is learned Héloïse,
For whom shorn Abélard was made
A tonsured monk upon his knees?
Such tribute his devotion paid.
And where's that queen who, having played
With Buridan, had him bagged and bound
To swim the Seine thus ill-arrayed?
But where shall last year's snow be found?

Queen Blanche the fair, whose voice could please
As does the siren's serenade,
Great Bertha, Beatrice, Alice—these,
And Arembourg whom Maine obeyed,
And Joan whom Burgundy betrayed
And England burned, and Heaven crowned:

Where are they, Mary, Sovereign Maid?
But where shall last year's snow be found?

Not next week, Prince, nor next decade,
Ask me these questions I propound.
I shall but say again, dismayed,
Ah, where shall last year's snow be found?

FRANÇOIS VILLON:
Ballade in Old French
(Car, ou soit ly sains apostolles)

Let it be Rome's great Pope, adored
Of all, in alb and amice dressed,
Who, girt with stole instead of sword,
Can knock the Devil galley-west,
By spite and sulphur unimpressed,
Yet he, like any poor valet,
Shall of this life be dispossessed.
Him too the wind shall blow away.

Be it Constantinople's lord,
The emperor of the golden fist,
Or that French king, whom Christ reward,
And whom of kings I count the best,
Since he to God (whose name be blest)
Built church and convent in his day.
Much fame he had, as books attest.
That too the wind shall blow away.

Grenoble's count, whom men accord
A wise head and a fearless breast,
What Dôle or Dijon can afford
Of nobles proud in shield and crest,
And such as jump at their behest,
Trumpeters, soldiers, footmen, they

Who stuff their guts with so much zest:
Them too the wind shall blow away.

Princes must die like all the rest,
Like all who are of mortal clay,
And should they grumble or protest,
That too the wind shall blow away.

FRANÇOIS VILLON:
A Ballade to End With

Here is poor Villon's final word;
The ink upon his will is dried.
Come see him properly interred
When by the bell you're notified,
And come in scarlet, since he died
Love's martyr, through his gentle heart:
This on one ball he testified
As he made ready to depart.

Nor do I think his claim absurd;
Love hounded him both far and wide,
By such contempt and malice spurred
That, clear to Roussillon, one spied
No thorn in all the countryside
But wore his tattered shirt in part.
So said he (and he never lied)
As he made ready to depart.

And thus and therefore it occurred
That one rag only clothed his hide
When he lay dead; what's more, we heard
How on his bed of death he cried
A pox on Love, who still applied,
Sharper than buckle-tongue, his dart

(A fact which left us saucer-eyed),
As he made ready to depart.

Prince, like a falcon in your pride,
Hear how his pilgrimage did start:
He swigged some dark-red wine, and sighed,
As he made ready to depart.

Notes

ON THE MARGINAL WAY. The reference is to George Borrow's *The Bible in Spain*, 1843, chapter 50.

IN THE FIELD. Some think that Euripides' lost play *Andromeda* told of the transformation of Andromeda—with Perseus, Cepheus, Cassiopeia, and Cetus—into the constellations bearing their names. See the *Oxford Classical Dictionary*, "Andromeda."

". . . beyond the limits we know, there is something boundless for our hearts." *A New Catechism*, p. 13.

A WOOD. The witch hazel's flowers come in fall, the petals often hanging on till spring.

RUNNING. April 19 is Patriots' Day in Massachusetts. On that day the Boston Marathon is run.

UNDER CYGNUS. Our solar system's movement toward Hercules is turned toward Cygnus by the rotation of the galaxy. The Swan, the Northern Cross, and the Sword are different names for the same constellation.

A RIDDLE. Answer: a campfire.

DEAD STILL. The seventeenth line ("Nothing is hidden that shall not be known") echoes Matthew 10:26, Mark 4:22, and Luke 8:17.

I am indebted, for linguistic and interpretive help, to Norman Thomas di Giovanni (*Everness, Ewigkeit*), Willis Barnstone (*Compass*), Olga Carlisle (the Akhmatova poem), and Max Hayward (the Voznesensky poems).

Distinguished books of poetry
available in paperbound editions
from Harcourt Brace Jovanovich, Inc.

Maxwell Anderson	*Four Verse Plays* (HB 25)
Aristophanes *(Fitts translations)*	*Four Comedies* (HB 51)
Wendell Berry	*Farming: A Hand Book* (HB 194)
Wolf Biermann	*The Wire Harp: Ballads, Poems, Songs* (HB 141)
Bertolt Brecht	*Selected Poems* (HB 195)
C. P. Cavafy	*The Complete Poems of Cavafy* (HB 108)
E. E. Cummings	*E. E. Cummings: A Selection of Poems* (HB 92)
	95 Poems (HPL 51)
	73 Poems (HPL 52)
T. S. Eliot	*The Cocktail Party* (HB 69)
	The Confidential Clerk (HB 70)
	The Family Reunion (HB 71)
	Four Quartets (HB 136)
	Murder in the Cathedral (HB 72)
	Old Possum's Book of Practical Cats (HPL 31)
	Selected Poems (HPL 21)
	The Waste Land and Other Poems (HB 1)
William Empson	*Collected Poems* (HB 38)